── **THE POWER OF** ──

BINK

*The New Movement
to Find Meaning
in 4 Easy Steps*

RICK MARTINEZ

THE POWER OF BINK

*The New Movement to Find
Meaning in 4 Easy Steps*

ISBN 978-1-6196133-0-0

LIONCREST
PUBLISHING

FOR LISA...

*"Let's sit on a
rooftop at 2 a.m.
and talk about life."*

CONTENTS

FOREWORD

BY SAM HORN

Like you, I suppose, I read—and write—to be inspired, to be caught up on new worlds, to have my imagination piqued, and to receive insights into how to be a better person.

Most of all, I read to be swept up in an incredibly well-told, original version of a universal story. That's what BINK is: an intriguing, original update of a universal story. In this case, the story is "How can I live a more meaningful, purposeful life?"

According to Rick Martinez, *finding* our purpose should not be our life's mission. That infers that our purpose is "out there" somewhere and that we're in constant search of it. That can be an exercise in frustration.

Rick's premise is this: "The key to a purposeful, well-led life is to live each moment more fully." Instead of asking ourselves the existential question *"Why* am I here?" which can lead to confusion and consternation, he suggests we ask, *"What does* this moment mean? *What could* it mean? *What* do I *want* it to mean?"

In other words, how do we add more meaning to our lives? By taking time to reflect upon, and recognize, the important BINK moments in our lives *as they're happening.*

Meaning is not "out there," waiting to be found. It's "in here," already embedded in our daily interactions, if we just notice them, imprint them, and are grateful for them.

Many of us have read books, attended seminars, and seen TED talks about people who tell us they have found their "life purpose." Singular. As if each of us has only one.

That belief can lead us to thinking, "Why haven't I found the *one* thing I was born to do that will make me happy, wealthy, and fulfilled?" That type of thinking can make us feel like losers in the life-purpose game.

Some people think, *Well, I've got a full-time job, bills to pay, and a family to feed. I don't have the time, energy, resources, or bandwidth to find my purpose. Maybe when I retire.* That type of thinking leaves us in limbo, perceiving that our dream life can only happen *after* we have more time, money, or freedom.

This book will help you revisit assumptions that may be keeping you from having the quality of life you want, need, and deserve. It introduces a set of actionable steps you can set in motion to integrate more meaning into your every day, starting today.

The good news is, as this book points out and as author George Elliot says, "It's never too late to become what you might have been." Read it and reap.

— SAM HORN, INTRIGUE EXPERT AND AUTHOR OF
POP! TONGUE FU! AND GOT YOUR ATTENTION?

CHAPTER 1

DISRUPT

*A journey is a person in itself; no two
are alike. And all plans, safeguards,
policing, and coercion are fruitless. We
find that after years of struggle that we
do not take a trip; a trip takes us.*

— JOHN STEINBECK

This book exists to talk about a little thing called the purpose of life. How does each of us find the unique purpose of our existence, our businesses, and our relationships? What is purpose, and how do we find it? How do we stay connected to it, experience it, and truly live it? And if we get knocked off course, how do we get back on?

A clearly defined purpose gives us energy, gives us meaning, and I would add that it even gives us power. Without it, we tend to drift and feel disconnected, or essentially, we let life live us instead of living the life we want. And I don't know about you, but letting life live me is not how I want to wake up every day. A life without a purpose can never be fulfilling. Relationships without a purpose drift apart. Companies without a purpose or a mission tend to wane. It's a bold claim to make, I know, but as this book unfolds for you, I know you'll begin to understand and feel the same way.

I know I have asked myself what my purpose is tons of times throughout my life: Why do I exist? Have *you*? I would imagine that if you are reading this book, then the answer is yes. Maybe even a "hell yes!" See, we've all done it!

No matter who you are, where you live, or what you do, we *all* ask this question. And perhaps this is why the all-important subject of purpose has been the focal point of so many books, seminars, lectures, and even religions. We are *constantly* seeking meaning in our lives—a reason for truly *living* life. The more meaning we have, the more purpose we have and the better our lives become.

I want to offer you a new way of looking at this subject. More significantly, I want to show you how to act on it.

CHAPTER 2

CRUSHED

Bad things do happen; how I respond to them defines my character and the quality of my life. I can choose to sit in perpetual sadness, immobilized by the gravity of loss, or I can choose to rise from the pain and treasure the most precious gift I have—life itself.

— WALTER ANDERSON

It started in September of 2012. When I say, "it started," I, of course, mean my awakening. My life. My mindfulness. With my BINK moment came my new beginning.

I was in Austin, Texas for a weight-lifting competition. The competition took place on a high school football field, and the day was perfect: no clouds...clear blue skies. I was well rested and mentally set to do great things that day. It felt like everything was coming together to set me up for success. I'm sure each of you has felt the same way at some point in your life. I'm sure your moment didn't come with a weight-lifting competition but perhaps within your job or your relationship—a moment in which everything felt oh so right. I felt tough, cool...unconquerable. And I was completely arrogant.

You see, I've always been a competitor. I pushed, I achieved, and I made it happen (no matter what "it" was), always setting myself up for the next challenge. That's how I found myself in this competition in the first place.

I was on top of the world after selling my company, which I'd spent fourteen years building, just a few months prior. I was ready to go after my next challenge, and this weight-lifting competition sounded like the perfect opportunity to score another win. (As I look back on how arrogant my thinking was then, it makes me sad and embarrassed.) I stepped to my first lift, and I hit it; in fact, I *nailed* it! I hit a personal record. Now I was really on top of the world. You see, for me, lifting weights isn't just about picking up pieces of iron; to me, it's the metaphor for life. Taking on the weight of the world, all our stresses, and all those problems, I feel that weight pushing down on me, and then I lift it off, becoming stronger. And right then, I felt the strongest I had ever been.

Now I really wanted to go for it. I added more weight to the bar and stepped up to the lift, figuring I was moments away from another PR. But once the bar was three to four feet off the ground, I knew something wasn't right. In that moment,

I *knew* it wasn't going to end well for me. And just like that, 225lbs came crashing down on my leg, and just as quickly, I came crashing down to the ground. My body collapsed in a heap, and my right leg couldn't move.

Time seemed to have slowed down. This had all happened in a matter of seconds—the lift had been fast, and the crash had been so much faster—but, in my mind, it felt like it had been hours. As I lay there on the ground, and just before the pain began to wash over me, I became fully present to the moment. (Searing physical pain has a way of doing that.) I had a moment of insight—a moment of reflection, a real reality check—and things became very focused. More than that, it was a moment of connectedness to life. In other words, I had a BINK. And it was not one of the subtle ones either. Just before the pain surged through me, I remember thinking to myself, *What are you supposed to do with this moment?*

Three months later, I was telling a good friend about my moment of clarity. I had a wine glass in my hand, and as I described how quickly my great day had turned terrible as the weight crashed down on my leg *like that,* I flicked the rim of the glass—BINK! The sound of my finger hitting the glass—BINK—chimed and resonated up into the air. It caught the attention of the people around us, and they moved in closer to listen. My friend looked around and said, "Rick, do you think that story could impact others? Could it change somebody's life if you told that story again? If you shared the insights you received, could it help folks make sense of their BINK moments and live a more purposeful life?"

I looked back at her pensively and said, "Yeah. Yes, I think it could." And right then and there, my story became a moral obligation to share, to connect, and to decipher exactly what these amazing moments are and how they can shape and change our worlds.

That's how BINK came about. It's a funny word; it's a sound that resonates and calls attention, just as our BINK moments call our attention to them. BINK is about being present, focused, and curious as we ask ourselves, *"What are you supposed to do with this moment?"*

"Why me?" was a question I asked myself again and again on that sunny day in Austin as I was crushed under physical and figurative weight. Months later, I realized the simple answer is that we all have our calling. We all have a moment or moments that define us, and it then becomes our decision to listen to and act on them. I've chosen to act.

And after reading this book, I believe you will too.

CHAPTER 3

LIGHT

It is good to have an end to journey toward;
but it is the journey that matters, in the end.

— ERNEST HEMINGWAY

To help as many people as possible, I am devoting myself to becoming the world's premier expert BINKologist. Of course, I say this with a smile, since BINKology isn't a field of study, and I certainly have no competition from fellow BINK experts. But joking aside, I have committed myself to understanding the unique capability of the human mind to deliver to us, from seemingly out of nowhere, breakthrough truths about ourselves that can awaken us with new energy, inspire us with new ideas, and open the doors to new opportunities for us.

In the time I have spent studying the art and science of

BINKology, I have learned a great deal, and I am excited and eager to share it. This book is the result of my study, and I offer you all that I have learned to inspire and awaken you, including the following:

- How to become more aware and attentive to those BINK moments
- How to process your BINKS in order to understand their meaning
- How to use your BINKS as the impetus to break away from the routines and habits that prevent you from pursuing your goals and changing your life for the better
- How to see your BINKS as stepping-stones toward aligning your passions, motivations, values, and desires in order to achieve your deepest, most cherished purpose in life.

This book aims to be pragmatic and straightforward. I am not a psychologist, therapist, or neuroscientist, so I won't be citing much in the way of theories and academic research. I write from my own experiences and those of hundreds of people I have interviewed about their BINK moments and the changes they made in their lives once they began listening closely to them.

This book is *not* a "follow your bliss book," and it is not *Life Purpose for Dummies*. While guiding you into understanding and unpacking your BINK moments, I will give you the tools you need to take action and implement the ideas and visions they provide you. I have created a powerful four-step BINK process map that helps you maximize the meaning of each BINK by being able to implement it in your life.

I hope you are already feeling inspired to start becoming the BINKologist of your own life. Perhaps you have already begun reflecting on a few of your most memorable BINKS. Are they flooding into your consciousness? Can you see the images in your mind from these past moments of clarity and break-through insight? Do you detect how they might even form a pattern for you, enabling you to discover who you are and what your life purpose must be? If you aren't yet, you will soon.

No matter your age, economic status, or educational back-ground, paying attention to your BINKS from this day forth will guide you to both inner wisdom and outer results that can transform you from feeling confused, stuck, unfulfilled, or lost to feeling confident, energized, engaged in life, and connected to your purpose. Your BINKS are the doorways to your future.

To adapt the famous Latin expression *carpe diem*—seize the day—I invite you to *carpe BINKUM*. Seize the BINK.

A final note and something to keep in mind are the various stages of comprehension: learning, growth, and mastery. When you take on a new task or learn a new process, such as learning to drive a car, you move through different levels of competence. In the beginning, you are ignorant...and blissfully so. Let's call it "unconsciously incompetent" (AKA you don't know what you don't know). Then you move to conscious incompetence, in which you've woken up to what you don't know. Remember that's an awakening that a BINK moment provides. Slowly, we build capability and become "consciously competent." This occurs after practice, practice, and more practice. The final stage is "unconscious competence" when, like an expert driver, this skill has become second nature, you can now do it with your eyes closed (though I certainly don't recommend that drivers do that!), and you are actually able to share and teach the skill to others.

Consider yourself at the first stage of an incredible experience and on a path to enlightenment. Your BINK moments and the BINK process will lead you to something very exciting.

CHAPTER 4

EMERGE

*The more you trust your intuition the more
empowered you become, the stronger you
become and the happier you become.*

— GISELE BÜNDCHEN

We've all had "those days." On any given day, you might be
running errands or grinding through your workday. Maybe
you're at school, pushing your way through "hump day" or
killing time on Facebook, and in the middle of that same old
routine, you have a feeling. It's a flutter in your stomach...a
sense of restlessness. Perhaps it's a distracting thought or a
slip of the tongue...a moment when you mean to say something predictable and it comes out provocative.

We've all had these moments. One second, we're moving

through our routine, our thoughts barely reaching beyond the next item on our to-do list, and then *BINK*, the next second, we're looking around at the life we've built for ourselves and saying, "This isn't right. Something's missing. Something's out of place."

We know we're supposed to do something different, but we're not sure what that "something" might be. It's a feeling—a certainty—we can't ignore.

- Some feel it in their gut and call it instinct.
- Some feel it in their head and call it an epiphany.
- Some feel it in their heart and call it intuition.
- Some feel it in their soul and call it a sign.

Whatever we call it, it's something that drives us to question our path...to take a second, third, or even fourth look at a situation. It prompts us to pause and reevaluate something that's going on at that moment.

The purpose of this book is to frame these events, instincts, epiphanies, intuitions, and signs as *BINK* moments. We'll also talk about what we're supposed to do with these *BINK* moments and why I feel it is so very important that we pay attention to them.

This book has been divided into short chapters so we can get to the point quickly and make the most use of your limited time. Each of these bite-size chapters comes with a different purpose (pun intended). After you have a firm understanding of what a *BINK* is, you can read each chapter independently and out of sequence if you choose to. This allows you to pick and choose your way through the book without losing something by changing the order, just as we do in life. We sometimes expect and often crave order, and yet, when reality hits, all of that goes out the window. There will also be real and true BINK stories sprinkled in from other people who have had a BINK moment, used the process, and emerged with a new perspective, deeper meaning, and true happiness. Pay attention to these, as they illustrate how the process works and unfolds in the real world.

Most of all, as you read this book, I encourage you to pay attention to your own BINK moments. Look for them in your past and present, listen to what these BINKS have to say to you, and consider whether or not you choose (or have chosen) to follow their advice.

CHAPTER 5

DEFINE

*When one door closes another door
opens, but we so often look so long and so
regretfully upon the closed door, that we
do not see the ones which open for us.*

— ALEXANDER GRAHAM BELL

What is a BINK?

A BINK is a life-changing moment that opens the door to what's next.

Short and sweet.

Our life experiences jump out to us as great Kodak moments. We Facebook them, Tweet them, blog them, and post them on YouTube. They document the sights and sounds of what we experience—the details that add flavor to our lives. But, more often than not, they are not moments that define us, change us, or show us new possibilities. They are interesting, even inspiring, but rarely do they push us beyond our comfort zone and into the unknown. When a life event goes beyond what is familiar, what is expected, or what we've prepared for, it may very well be a BINK moment.

A BINK is a life-changing moment that opens the door to what's next.

For a second, let's pretend that one of those moments has just happened. It is usually only one of two types: obvious or subtle.

Sometimes, they just sneak up on us in a gentle, tugging way, and at other times, they are plainly visible—maybe a slap in the face, a push, a pull, or even a shove.

So ask yourself: When a BINK happens, does it feel like a life experience? In other words, when these moments happen, do you see a door?

On this door, there is a sign that says "ENTER FOR MORE," and this door is cracked open ever so slightly. There is a little light shining through the crack, surrounding the doorframe in an inviting way. You see it, and more so, you *feel* it. As your gaze shifts downward, you notice an arrow on the ground at the door's threshold. It is pointing to the door—almost *through* the door—and into the light. And on the arrow, it says, "WHAT'S NEXT?"

This is a life-changing moment. The door now opens. You don't even need to push it open because it's going to happen whether you know it or like it. The only question is what will happen next. It's always our decision whether we look through the door and take the next step to cross its threshold and discover what's next or whether we step back, put our heads down, and walk right past it. It's our choice. It's *your* choice. That's the definition of a BINK—a life-changing moment that opens the door to what's next.

Does it sound familiar? Does it feel familiar?

As the book evolves and as your story unfolds, you will see how important these BINK moments really are and how the failure to listen to them could be catastrophic. They could take us away from opportunity. They could take us further away from the things that are most important to us—and, sometimes, without us ever even knowing. It's a sad thing to think about. Imagine going through your *entire life* unconsciously incompetent.

One story might not be enough to prove to you that BINKS exist, but what about ten? Twenty? One hundred? I bet that if you start asking around—asking the people you're close to about moments in their lives that defined who they are and where they're going—every single one of them will be able to tell you a story about a moment in which they chose to accept a challenge that life threw at them or a moment in which they chose to back away.

CHAPTER 6

EXIST

In theory, there is no difference between
theory and practice. In practice there is.

— YOGI BERRA

Some people seem to be born with a sense of purpose and a clear direction in life. But more and more often, we see people lost, leading lives of not only what Thoreau would call "quiet desperation" but also lives of loud distraction. This is due to a lack of purpose. They are glued to their cell phones, which act as electric leashes pulling them out of the moment. They are wasting their time—and, therefore, their lives—by sitting in front of the TV, surfing the Internet, feeling depressed, and eating for entertainment. They are doing their work not to add value or gain new skills but just to pay the bills and go through the motions.

Even in our own lives, we can relate to this at times. We see that without a clear outcome, our productivity tends to lessen. Our relationships lose energy. Without a sense of purpose, we drift and meander. Just as the unfocused mind wanders, a life without purpose leads us astray. Some folks never truly seem to find out who they are or what they are made of. They haven't had the experiences that give them that meaning they are looking for. Or, sometimes, we find someone who once thought they had this purpose thing all figured out. Then life happened. They had an experience—a BINK that knocked them off track: They got sick, a loved one died, or their business suffered a financial setback. *Something* happened. And now they feel lost. These experiences in life are calling us to an evolving purpose. But if we don't hear the call... if we don't fully process the experience—the BINK—then we get stuck...stuck in life, stuck in our heads, and driven to distraction...off course and off purpose.

What have those BINK moments meant to you? Many people find meaning in life from activities such as those involving religion, family, exercise, or music—anything that allows you to pursue your passions. Isn't that wonderful? There are so many possible paths. What's your life purpose? To inspire others to reach their highest potential? To promote a greener, more eco-friendly world? To help others heal through yoga? Whatever it is, a life filled with meaning, fulfillment, and purpose could mean a longer life.

A group of researchers at the Rush Alzheimer's Disease Center in Chicago tracked hundreds of people with an average age of eighty for seven years, assessing their physical, psychological, and cognitive well-being. At the beginning of the study, the participants were scored on their sense of purpose, using statements such as "Some people wander aimlessly through life, but I am not one of them" and "I sometimes feel as if I have done all there is to do in life." The study participants who had a higher sense of purpose were 2.4 times less likely to develop Alzheimer's than their lower-scoring peers. This held true even if their brains showed physical signs of the disease. "Even for people developing plaques and tangles in their brains, having a purpose in life allows you to tolerate them and still maintain your cognition," says neuropsychologist Patricia Boyle, the author of the study, which was published in the *Archives of General Psychiatry*.

The perks of purpose don't stop there. Purposeful people also had a 30% lower rate of cognitive decline, a lower risk of diabetes, and less likelihood of dying. People "want to make a contribution," says Boyle. "They want to feel part of something that extends beyond themselves...a sense of their role in the community and the broader world."

I can hear some folks now: "But that'll never happen to me, Rick, because I'm young, I'm working, and I'm too busy to be thinking about turning eighty!"

Well then, let me share another tidbit of info with you:

In a different study, Gallup's 2013 *State of the American Workplace Report* had grim results, including that 70% of the folks surveyed either hated their work or were completely disengaged, and perks didn't help. *Seventy* percent! Other results of this survey weren't much better. At best, only 30% of the 150,000 full- and part-time workers surveyed honestly enjoyed their jobs and their bosses.

And that's where the good stuff stops.

See, a full 20% of those responding are classified as "actively disengaged," meaning these are the ones who are muttering complaints at the water cooler and using break time to check out job postings online.

The remaining 50% of US workers polled are classified as merely "disengaged," meaning they may show up to work but are not really showing up with energy or to make an effort.

Of all the studies and stats on purpose, meaning, and happiness, these two struck a chord with me. Yet, on the bright side, you can reap the benefits of knowing and living your life's purpose at any age. It's never too late...or too early. As the Roman philosopher Seneca said, "It is not that we have so little time but that we lose so much...The life we receive is not short but we make it so; we are not ill provided but use what we have wastefully."

When someone lives a life of purpose, they produce. When someone lacks purpose, they tend to consume. They are looking to fill that void, and in doing so, what they consume often ends up consuming them. It may consume their entire life. This is not a purposeful existence. We see it in the home, in business, and in relationships, and it only seems to be getting worse.

CHAPTER 7

WORTH

Believe in yourself and all that you are.
Know that there is something inside
you that is greater than any obstacle.

— CHRISTIAN D. LARSON

You may already be successful, or have experienced success, and now find yourself asking, "Is this all there is?" Maybe you've found yourself in a golden handcuff position—you don't like your life or job, but you have to pay the mortgage and keep the lights on. Perhaps you feel like this is the hand you've been dealt and there's nothing you can do about it. Maybe you know what you want to do, but you just don't know *how* to do it. Whatever it is, or whatever it seems to be, you are not alone in thinking this. I know this from experience.

These are some of the questions I started asking myself, and they are questions for you to also ask yourself as you consciously examine the BINKS in your own life:

"What will happen if I do this?"

"What will happen if I don't do this?"

"What won't happen if I do this?"

"What won't happen if I don't do this?"

It was through this internal dialogue—a mental question-and-answer game—that I started to rethink what things meant...or what they were supposed to mean. It was through this process that I began to really wrap a new consciousness around events that were happening in my life. Instead of asking *why*, I began to ask *what*. *What* does this mean to me is so different from *why* did this happen to me?

Then, one day, I found myself looking in the mirror, and as I stared back at myself, I said,

"If not you, then who?" I realized that a fulfilled and bountiful life was right up ahead and available in ways I never imagined possible. And I asked, "Yeah, why not me?"

So, the bigger question is, "Why not you?"

Curiosity is a fantastic starting point. I want to challenge you to clear out of your mind any and all preconceived notions of what finding your life purpose is, what discovering a life of fulfillment should be, and what the most recent study on happiness says you must do. It's clutter. Clear it out now. Come with an open mind, an open heart, and a spirit that is prepared to revel and to receive, and make it your intent to start paying attention to what you want to attract into your life.

It starts with BINKS. It always has. It always will.

And now I want to share a story about why it is so important to not wait.

CHAPTER 8

HINDSIGHT

Again and again, the impossible problem
is solved when we see that the problem is
only a tough decision waiting to be made.

— ROBERT H. SCHULLER

About nine years ago, I was working in a busy ER. This was nothing new; I had worked in a slew of busy ERs and trauma centers since becoming a registered nurse in 1995. But this night shift was remarkable because of one special patient.

It was just after 11:30 p.m. on a random weeknight. Our EMS phone rang, and the paramedic let us know they were headed our way. We could hear the sirens in the background, and as he gave us a report, the words we heard were "heart attack." Those two words lit us up.

The ambulance pulled in, and the medics wheeled in a fifty-nine-year-old guy. One look at this guy and you could tell he was a dad. He was wearing a polo shirt, cargo shorts, and moccasin-like slippers (the kind dads wear around the house). It was also easy to see that this guy—this *dad*—was scared for his life.

We slid him onto our hospital gurney and set to work. We started a second IV, put the electrode patches on his chest so we could see his heart rhythm, strapped on the blood pressure cuff, and let the IVs drip. It was very methodical, much like one would see on TV. As I worked on him, I caught a quick sideways glance at his face, and I saw his fear. I saw him close his eyes and swallow really hard, trying to hold back tears. We all kept on working.

The machines chirped. The doctor called out orders. The X-ray crew barreled into the room. We all kept on working.

Then his family arrived: his daughter, with a baby in her arms; his son; and his wife.

I could see how scared they were as well. I saw his wife crying. I saw his daughter holding his grandson a little closer. I saw his son place his face in his hands, his chest rising and falling a little deeper. In fact, the overwhelming feeling of *Is Dad leaving us?* was so heavy that we could *all* feel it. It settled over the room like a thick wool blanket on a 110-degree summer day. We all kept on working.

I had a moment then: I felt myself zoom out, as if I were taking in the scene from above in an observant, disassociated way. As I took in this surreal reality, I saw the team as we continued to work to inject drugs into the IVs and to ask him questions about his medical history and whether he took any medications. I "saw" that this was more than a patient and an ER; it was a BINK unfolding right before my eyes.

Then it got real.

He turned his head toward his family and continued to answer our questions. I could see a tear roll down the side of his cheek as he turned away. He then said in a rather shaky voice, "Well, I've been pretty healthy. Though I was at my doc's office just six months ago, and he recommended I prioritize my health more. You know, cut back on crazy work hours, rest more, exercise more, and eat healthier because I was a walking time bomb." He went on to say, "And I looked at him and thought to myself, *Sure, doc, you just don't understand how crazy busy my life is.* I told him that I would make some changes, but in reality, I didn't."

Then he paused, turned his head back to us, tried to smile, and said, "I guess I should have listened. I guess I should've taken action six months ago."

You see, BINK moments happen whether we want them to or not. These moments offer us an opportunity, sometimes very subtly, and at other times, they come as an earth-shattering experience. It's truly up to us to heed them, honor them, process them, and allow them to mold and shape our lives to be more fulfilling and purpose-driven. The story I shared is one

I'll never forget because, that night, I realized that *my* "six months ago" also began.

So, as we consider these moments and ponder what these BINKS *do* offer, think of this day as the start of your "six months ago." What will you do differently tomorrow?

Will you ignore the subtle BINKS and allow them to change into obvious, possibly catastrophic ones? Or will you be more aware and curious about your BINKS?

Thankfully, our patient came out of his BINK okay. I surely hope his realization that night compelled him to make positive changes in his life—the changes that, as we all know, will only happen if we *choose* to take action toward them. Remember: Not acting is also a choice.

Your six months ago starts now.

CHAPTER 9

CONNECT

*Too often we underestimate the power of
a touch, a smile, a kind word, a listening
ear, an honest compliment, or the
smallest act of caring, all of which have
the potential to turn a life around.*

— LEO BUSCAGLIA

There is no doubt that we are in an era of mindfulness. There is a new and growing social consciousness that is transcending the individual you and me. It is a feeling of connectedness not only to each other but also to things that are bigger than we all are individually. We see it every day all around us. From the story of the lady at Starbucks in St. Petersburg, Florida who started an "acts of kindness chain" by buying the coffee for the person behind her in the drive-through, setting off a chain reaction of 378 pay-it-forward coffee purchases. We see it in entrepreneurism with companies such as BANGS Shoes. BANGS has made it its mission to invest 20% of net profits with entrepreneurs through its nonprofit partner, Kiva. Also worthy of note is the Giving Pledge. This is a commitment by the world's wealthiest individuals and families to dedicate the majority of their wealth to philanthropy. These people, events, and endeavors all started with a single moment—a BINK that led to a bigger picture.

The fact is that many of us, including me, procrastinate. We think things such as "I'll live my life and heed those moments when I retire," "when the kids go off to school," or "when I make more money." This kind of procrastination is all many of us have known up until now. But consider this: Choosing to continue to think and act in this fashion is essentially choosing a life that will lead to regret. One of the purposes of this movement is to guide you into taking action *now*—to follow your BINKS and build the life you choose.

Why wait to get started? *Now* is the perfect time. The human race is beginning to connect in ways we never thought or imagined possible.

It's not just about me.

It's not just about you.

It's about all of us. We are interconnected and doing incredible things together by allowing our BINKS to enrich our lives in ways we never knew were possible.

You have the resources you need to achieve your desired outcomes. Resources can be internal beliefs, energy, and personal skills, as well as people, possessions, money, and, of course, the BINK process.

So, if not now, when?

CHAPTER 10

BANGS

All of our reasoning ends in surrender to feeling.

— BLAISE PASCAL

Hannah Davis is the founder of one of the coolest companies around. After getting to know her and her remarkable story, I was lucky enough to secure a short interview with her about how it all started. And it started with a BINK.

The following are Hannah's words:

I don't know if I'll ever be able to forget my BINK moment. I was twenty-two years old, teaching English in China for a year. I had just graduated from Clemson University with a political science degree and a minor in Mandarin, and if you had told me at that

BANGS · 45

time I would be involved in business as the founder of a shoe com-
pany, I probably would have laughed at you. But I did always
know that I wanted to work in the social sector, potentially in
development. I also knew that I wanted to work with an organi-
zation that furthered some type of cause; I just wasn't sure how
that was going to pan out.

While I was in China, I noticed a pair of olive green shoes worn by
Chinese workers and farmers. It was super simple, classic canvas,
and really easy to wear. The timing couldn't have been better either:
Other companies in the market were finding success in linking each
sale of their product to a give-back initiative. I loved that concept
and decided to move forward with what would become BANGS
Shoes. The word "Bangs" comes from the word "help" in Manda-
rin. So when you buy a pair of BANGS *Shoes, we help people start*
businesses all over the world. The beautiful and unique part of this
model is that it was founded on the idea that if you give a man a
fish, he eats for a day, but if you teach a man to fish, he eats for a
lifetime. So, the entire model is about helping people help themselves.

My entire business can trace back to a single moment—my BINK.
I was sitting in my room on my bed, and I literally sat up and said,
"Oh my gosh, it's the shoes!" and everything kind of grew from
there. In the past two years, we have been able to grow a college
program on over forty campuses across the country with 250 stu-
dents involved. We've been able to invest in many entrepreneurs
in nineteen countries (including the US) and in many different
sectors. It's been a really, really exciting time, and it all started
with a BINK *and the decision to act on it.*

Hannah's story is an awesome illustration of the lasting impact of a single moment—not just in her life, but also in the lives of the entrepreneurs BANGS Shoes has invested in. It's a perfect example of the importance of listening to your BINKS.

CHAPTER 11

EVOLVE

Thinking: the talking of the soul with itself.

— PLATO

In learning more about this subject, I picked up a copy of *The Purpose Driven Life*, one of the most-purchased books over the past decade. And in this book, the author, Rick Warren, attempts to explain why we are here and aims to help us find our purpose through spirituality. More to the point, the book offers a forty-day spiritual journey through which we learn to answer the question, "What on earth am I here for?" In another amazing book, *Man's Search for Meaning*, Holocaust survivor Viktor Frankl recounts his harrowing escape from a Nazi concentration camp. He discovered that it was, in fact, purpose that determined whether he would survive or perish. He escaped from what most of us would consider Hell, running over seventy miles naked in the cold to escape, and he eventually went on to start his own practice as a therapist. Frankl developed a type of analysis called logotherapy, which is based on the belief that striving to find meaning in one's life is the most powerful motivating and driving force in a human being. In Napoleon Hill's famous book *Think and Grow Rich*, Hill conducted a twenty-year study in which he detailed the psychology of 504 of the most successful people of his time: Henry Ford, Thomas Edison, Roosevelt, the Wright brothers, Schwab, Carnegie, and on and on. Through this study, he found that a definite purpose in life topped the list as the single most determining factor in a person's success, happiness, achievement, and fulfillment.

As you can see, there have been countless books written about purpose and how some people have found it. All these books and their authors are spot on in what they propose: They each talk about the ways in which they reached their ultimate purpose and how they discovered a fulfilled life. And from these, we all get a sense of what it means to find your purpose and realize its importance. I respect each and every person who has ever written of and shared their path to uncovering their purpose, but there has never been a road map—a clear system to help us navigate our own path to purpose. None of the past and recent studies, books, literature, or otherwise talk about a common and shared method to actually discover one's very own purpose in life.

Until now.

I want to show you that map, and even more so, I want to show you why it matters, why this is the time to do it, and why it is important for *you* to live fulfilled. I'll invite you to think about some of your most life-changing experiences today. These pivotal experiences that impact our lives are BINKS. These are experiences we've all had that open the door to what's next; they open the door to our personal evolution. However, it's up to us to walk through that door, as you will see as you read on.

Also, if you are going through a tough time right now because of something that has happened in the past or continues to be a challenge—in your business, relationships, health, or any area of your life—not only will you be able to see where you may be off, but you will also see what it takes to get back on the path to experiencing life more meaningfully.

I believe *all of us,* at some point in our lives, have felt lost or have been faced with a life-changing moment that made us question our purpose, our existence, and our reason for existing or just led us to just ask questions. For some, it's a consistent thought, while for others, the search for purpose is more like background noise that manifests as a life without true meaning, a life that has them simply going through the motions, and a dispassionate life that seems to whisper, "What's the point in trying?"

As our research and the BINK process unfolded, we quickly discovered that purpose is often a moving target. Let that sink in for a moment. Purpose is a moving target; it's not the ultimate end game. Consider a soldier who returns home from war; his purpose is no longer to fight that battle, but a new purpose unfolds from a new experience and from a new inter-action, leading him in a new direction. But if this soldier gets lost in the past and is not present in the moments happening in the here and now, he will remain at war. Life will always be a battle for him, even if the battle is solely with himself.

We are *all* on a path, a journey, or a mission, if you will. But what happens once the mission is over? How do we shape and remold our identities, our characters, and our purposes in life to fit with our highest values? How do we discover a new mission, a new direction, or an evolved purpose?

The more I spoke to and listened to individuals of all shapes, sizes, creeds, colors, and religions, the more I began to see a pattern emerge. It wasn't so much about differentiating between successful people and unsuccessful people. And it wasn't so much about understanding why some people are more driven than others. It was actually much more simple than that.

It was about how some people took those BINK moments and truly did something with them. But even more drilled down were the actions they pragmatically took to actualize the moment. It's a bold proposition, I know, and over the last few years, we have indeed shown that this process works. It's not about the end state; it's about the moments and understanding what they mean to us.

Project BINK is not just about learning new information. It's not about me teaching you what purpose is and why it's important, because information is rarely ever what changes your life. It's *experience*! It's your BINKS. We can all think of experiences that have forever changed our lives. These experiences are what will open the door to what's next in your purpose and personal evolution; so, this book is about learning how to process them.

The road map will show you a new way of looking at purpose—not as a destination in itself but, rather, as a path to fulfillment based on your personal experiences and life-defining moments. You've heard that it's all about the journey, not the destination. Well, I also want you to think about this: It's progress that leads to happiness. It's not always the achievement in and of itself but the feeling that we are going somewhere...that we are progressing in our lives. From business to relationships, health, progress, and growth, progress allows us to feel more alive.

And when we feel like our progress has stopped, we start to feel unhappy. This is why we see people who seemingly have it all end up depressed. If you feel like you're at the top, if you have achieved your purpose, what else is there to look forward to? If your purpose is getting to the moon and you get there, then you have nothing to look forward to unless you find your next purpose. This is part of the reason why our goals and purpose *must* evolve.

Through this process, I am inviting you to explore more deeply and systematically the experiences that have shaped you and those yet to come that will indeed continue to mold you. You may begin to think about what led you to start your company, perhaps start a relationship, or even end one: a health crisis, a child being born, moving, joining a new organization, a car accident, or an adventure? What led you to this day? I want you to think about those BINKS, both subtle and obvious, that brought you to where you are right now.

So, can you think about experiences in your life that have shaped where you are today?

These life-changing moments open the door to what's next; it's these BINKS that lead us to our purpose. It's the BINKS that are guiding us to our purpose, and how fulfilled, purposeful, and successful you feel your life is today is based on how well you *have* or *have not* processed these BINKS.

There are little BINKS happening all the time and big BINKS that *completely* change our lives in an instant. In the forthcoming chapters, we'll dive a little deeper into the process.

So now let's dig in.

CHAPTER 12

PRESENCE

Life is available only in the present moment. If you abandon the present moment you cannot live the moments of your daily life deeply.

— THICH NHAT HANH

BINK PROCESS STEP 1

The message I'm about to share has already impacted over half a million lives of people all over, including those from big organizations, such as the American Diabetes Association and the Meals on Wheels Association of America. After seeing firsthand how BINK has helped people find purpose in their lives, I am excited to have the opportunity to share it with you.

Many, if not all, of us would like to be more present in life so that we don't miss it as it happens and so that we can enjoy it more fully and in the manner that this wonderful existence can offer. So let me give you a quick illustration. And because I love to eat, let's use food as our example. Imagine having a fantastic meal in front of you, and as you begin to eat, you start thinking about work. As you chew your first bite, that unanswered email starts to gnaw at you. You focus on the conversations of your workday and the unchecked boxes on your to-do list, and then you look down at your plate: Your food is gone. You ate it all without tasting a bite. Has that ever happened to you?

When you allow your mind to wander back into the past or ahead into the future, you miss out on the flavors of your meal. You miss out on the conversation with your kids, as well as on your spouse's smile. Now imagine you could give your dinner your full attention; you take in the aromas, the taste of the first bite, and the funny story your kid tells about his day at school. It's then and only then that you fully appreciate the dish...the moment.

Life works the same way. We are so obsessed with thinking about other things that our monkey minds take over, and we can't be present in the moment. And as it always happens, in a snap, the moment has passed. We can learn to let go of this type of thinking, however, and be more present.

The essence of this step is creating versus reacting. When you experience a BINK, the first thing you should think is, *What do I want to create from this?* versus *Am I going to allow this to create me?* Now let's follow the *process.*

I had a life-changing moment—a BINK—when the weight crashed down on me. I got present and fully associated. I could have tuned out (dissociated), as I touched on earlier. I could have numbed myself with beer, pain pills, TV, or the Internet. I had every excuse in the book to turn in that direction, especially after such a hefty event and injury. I could have distracted myself. But, instead, I got really present with the pain. Not only the pain in the moment but the pain that followed. It wasn't just physical pain that I became present to but also emotional and psychological pain. My injury was a major blow to my ego.

And here's the thing: In life, our egos will get bruised, and we then have the choice to create or to react. The day will come when the ego is healed, and then who will show up? What will show up? And why? If we don't choose to listen to our BINKS, it will be the same person as before. So put the ego aside and get present, because once we realize that the ego is out of the way, the only option left is to take the next step. This step into the unknown can be a scary proposition, and that's okay. We are all scared until the day we are not. In getting present, I found that we all have some pain in our lives: emotional pain, financial pain, stress, loss, or relationship pain. It was a simple distinction but, for me, a profound one. I felt a sense of connectedness in that moment—a universal connection through experiences...through BINKS. It was a life-changing moment, and I really got present to it.

Getting Centered: Steps to Becoming Present

Find Quiet: Quieting your thoughts is an ideal way to get in touch with your unconscious mind and open the floodgates of creativity. Now before we go on, let me stress that I'm not speaking about painting, acting, or reading poetry; those are creative acts, of course, but I'm talking about creativity in your own life. It is my hope that you will begin to see a BINK moment for what it truly is and that you will begin to create the masterpiece that is your life the way you know it should and could be. One of the best ways of doing this is by building some quiet time into your life in order to meditate, contemplate, think, ponder, or pray. This quiet time allows you to use your mind instead of your mind using you all day.

Build a Ritual: A great way to train your unconscious mind is to have a ritual in place. Setting up a ritual of lighting candles, dimming the lights, and turning on music to relax and calm your overactive brain is a great way to get into the process of quieting down. The things I just described are actually part of my everyday evening ritual as I unplug from the craziness of the day and plug into the calm that the evening will bring. To get yourself started, set aside a space in a room—or, if you're able to, an entire room—that your unconscious mind associates with quiet time and peace, or find a spot for yourself outside. The important thing is that you designate your spot with the specific purpose of finding peace and quiet.

Include an Hour of Power: One of my other centering habits is that I start each day with an hour of power. It includes time to reflect on the previous day, to read something inspirational that morning, and to let myself know that, regardless of how yesterday was, today is a fresh start. For me, it is very invigorating and hugely motivating. I approach each day refreshed and ready to tackle the world. A physical routine makes it much easier to build the habit to become present. The gift of this type of daily ritual is that once it becomes habit, we are better able to work with our BINKS. As BINK moments occur, it will be nearly seamless to get into this state of receiving what the BINK is saying.

Meditate: Meditation is powerful, and it's not just for spirituality anymore. Better yet, this amazing tool doesn't require any special equipment, books, videos, or high-priced courses. It just requires your willingness and desire to want to quiet your mind and become present. Meditation is good for productivity and for creativity as well. It also comes with an amazing potential side effect: an increase in your happiness factor! Of all the reasons one should meditate, perhaps my favorite is the fact that it allows me the opportunity to connect with something bigger than me.

So, here are some easy and practical ways to start meditating *now*:

1. Ask yourself why you are meditating. To start the day? To begin to process a BINK moment? Perhaps to end the day? Use that reason as a starting point.
2. Commit to start. Give yourself just five minutes and commit 100% to that time. No ifs, ands, or buts; commit to start. This commitment is essential.
3. Sit with a strong physiology: no slumping shoulders or

passive energy. And on the flipside, there's no need to sit up like a flagpole either. Sit in a way that is pleasantly confident, and let it feel natural.

4. Focus on a picture in your mind or on a mantra. It could be the image of a sailboat sailing gently across the sea, or it could be a mantra, such as "Today is the first day of the rest of my life. Today it begins anew."

5. "Un-focus" happens. It will happen. You will see the sailboat in your mind then start to think about dinner. No worries. Just refocus on the image or mantra. It's that simple. Your mind *will* wander, so accept it, refocus, and gently bring yourself back to your image, mantra, or simply just your breathing.

6. Be patient. We tend to be our own worst critics and judges. Get over it. Just commit to showing up daily and without fail. Be consistent and persistent, and just like anything else in life, you will be successful.

7. Remember. Remember that it's not about the five minutes, the mantra, or the sailboat; rather, it's about how it will make you feel for the rest of the day, the tone it will set, and the BINK that will be processed.

Because, as we've discussed, BINK moments speak.

Your BINK moments are doing their best to show you something and are attempting to guide you. Learn to listen to what your BINKS are saying, and if your conscious mind wants to take over and react (like it often will and does), direct your unconscious mind gently to get it to do what you want. You can then have the positive outcome you are craving. By going back again and again to your well-formed outcome, you train your unconscious mind to work with you in achieving your goal. Step 1 in the BINK process is your guide. Once you are present to the moment and ready to continue processing the BINK, it's now time for Step 2.

CHAPTER 13

MEANING

*If you change the way you look at
things, the things you look at change.*

— WAYNE DYER

BINK PROCESS STEP 2

After my BINK, and after I fully embraced what it means to
be present and that I was ready to create the rest of my life, I
then moved into Step 2 of the BINK process. I made it mean
something. Looking for meaning in our actions is something
we all do. Human beings are meaning-making machines. We
make everything mean *something*. But realize this: Nothing has
any meaning except for the meaning we give it.

For example, let's say you are scheduled to go on a date. You leave work on time, race home to get ready, are about to step outside, and you receive a call: Your date cancels. Immediately, you are filled with emotions, and with these emotions, you can create either positive or negative meanings. You may find yourself flooded with immediate disappointment—maybe even anger at the situation—wondering why the universe decided to ruin an otherwise great day. Or perhaps you experience disappointment, but you understand that things change, and you let the cancellation roll off your back. In either case, you took a moment and made it mean something. Can you recall an experience like this in your life? Perhaps where you reacted and applied a meaning only to later find that the exact opposite was the truth?

From the same experience, we can have different emotions and, therefore, different meanings. When we become fully present to an experience like Step 1 demands, we create meaning for it that either empowers or disempowers us. This means we can take a BINK—or any moment, for that matter—and make it work for us or make it work against us.

I decided to give my BINK moment an empowering meaning. I chose to grow in my compassion for others. I chose to grow stronger emotionally. I chose to share it with others as I have done in this book. In short, a truly empowering meaning should make you feel good; it should be something that's good for you and for those around you. It should connect to something bigger.

As you move forward on the journey from where you are to

where you want to be, you are going to have to confront some of the fears that perhaps your BINKS will drive to the surface: the fear of massive change or the fear of chasing your dreams. Fear is just a natural part of living; don't let it stand in your way.

Whenever you start a new project, take on a new venture, or put yourself out there, as often our BINKS tell us to do, there's usually *some* fear involved. Unfortunately, most people let fear stop them from taking the necessary steps to achieve their dreams.

Confronting your fears is a very necessary step in achieving success and meaning. In fact, it is the place where it begins.

So, as an example, let's say your BINK moment happens and you move on to Step 2. The BINK you experienced and the subsequent information then passes through the following filters:

- Your current world map or how you view the world
- Values
- Beliefs
- Decisions
- Memories

This results in an internal representation of the event within you; in other words, this is where you give the BINK meaning. But the whole intent of this step in the BINK process is to create and apply the meaning you want to give it, like I did in my example. When you do, you then create within you a state of being that combines your mental and physical states to move in a positive direction. In simpler terms, you get to give it an empowering meaning.

There is simply no other way.

Self-Limiting Beliefs

What happens next usually leads to a self-limiting belief. The BINK has spoken, and because of our filters, we might say, do, or think the following:

- Making money is always a struggle...
- I'm not important enough...
- Good-looking men (or women) are never nice to me...
- I'm too old (or I'm too young)...
- People won't take me seriously...
- I'm a bad writer...
- I don't deserve it...
- People from where I'm from are always poor...
- Problems always follow me...
- I never have good luck...
- And on and on and on...

These types of beliefs are generally showstoppers, and yet I'm here to say they don't need to be, nor should they be.

So how do we turn off these beliefs? How do we flip them into positives, begin to crush our fears, and give our BINKS (and hence our lives) the meaning they deserve? How do we give them the meaning that will move us forward and closer to a fulfilled life and deeper purpose? It's always easy to just talk about crushing fear or having a positive mind-set, but without a practical tool, it's truly just words on a page. It's nothing more than a great story of "how that other guy did it."

So here's something to sink your chops into: a quick exercise—one of many in the BINK toolkit—to start this baby moving:

1. Define your limiters

Think about your own limiting beliefs, fears, and things holding you back. Then write them down in much the way I just did above. Keep it simple, on a sheet of paper or your laptop, and write out four to five bullet points.

2. Flip it on its head

Pick just one of the bullet points that you just wrote down and let's work on one at a time. Look for *one* specific example in which your limiting belief is just not true. This rebuttal may come from your experience or someone else's.

As an example: If my belief is "I can't write," I might recall an article I wrote that was published in a popular fitness magazine. Or if I tell myself "People from where I'm from are always poor," I can recall a good friend of mine who lived in housing projects, grew up, and started his own successful company.

What Step 2 does here is let us know that there exists a possibility that these beliefs are just not universally true and that they may indeed be flawed. From this point forward, as you plow through your day, begin to look for examples that flip your self-limiting belief on its head.

3. Recreate the feeling

Ask yourself, how does the limiting belief make me feel? Perhaps it makes you feel heavy in some parts of your body. Think of the moments when this belief worked against you or when perhaps it held you back from making the move or taking the step you knew you should be taking. It could have been a relationship, a job, or your health and fitness perhaps. How has it hurt you? Write this down. If you wish to take this a little deeper, close your eyes and imagine the pain you experienced as a result of this belief. Think about the pictures, the sounds, and the emotions. Make it as real as possible.

4. Get to the root

Where did the belief come from? Was it from your childhood? Maybe your teen years? Dig deep into your memory bank and search for the root...for the source. When you capture it, write that down. Try to be specific, truthful, and clear, and use as many words and descriptors as you need to fully embrace the root. As a quick tip, doing these exercises often has better results when you have time to think and process freely, often with your eyes closed. A quiet place and blocked time works well for me. Capture the essence of the emotion and how it made you feel. Some simple descriptors could be *mad, sad, glad, afraid,* or *ashamed.*

5. Give it a new meaning

If in Step 4, you recalled a specific event, please know that this "event" isn't necessarily responsible for the ensuing belief, but the meaning we attached to it is. For instance, if in the 7th grade, my teacher gave me a poor grade on an essay, it didn't mean I had to create this limiting belief that I am a bad writer. It is because that was how I interpreted it, and in turn, that was the meaning I gave to that grade and my ability.

We can give any meaning we want to any situation, and I chose one that was limiting. In doing so, I gave it power.

So as a practical application, ponder the limiters in your life, and think about what alternative meanings you can apply to them. View them from different perspectives, from different angles, and even from different emotional standpoints. In my example, some potential alternatives were that perhaps my teacher was going through a divorce or having a rough day. Or, heck, maybe it was just a one-off occurrence.

Now, close your eyes and view the scene again—only, this time, with the new perspective...with the alternative meaning. This is the power of applying the meaning that you choose to apply! Doesn't it feel different, positive, and more empowering?

I bet it does.

6. Kiss your limiters goodbye

The final step is to fully awaken and ask yourself how you feel now.

Once you have fully processed and understood the importance of meaning and self-empowerment, then you are ready for the next step in the BINK process.

CHAPTER 14

CREATE

*Accept—then act. Whatever the present
moment contains, accept it as if you had
chosen it. Always work with it, not against it.*

— ECKHART TOLLE

BINK PROCESS STEP 3

If the first two steps in the process are inward or "states of
being," then the next two are outward or "states of doing." It
matters, because once you've recognized your BINK, honored
it, and then given it an impactful meaning, it's time to take
action. This is where the rubber meets the road. The action
we take will ultimately move our lives forward or backward.
And, remember, taking no action is still an action. There are

so many ways to deal with the challenges that come into our lives: Some people drink, some go for a run, and some sit around and cry. But some cry and then go start a foundation, some run a marathon, and some raise money for cancer; some *watch* TV, and others *make* TV shows. In other words, some people *react* while others *create*.

In the action stage, this is where we say (based on the experience that we are fully present to and the meaning we have given it), *I am going to do* _____. Again, the action could be positive or negative—another step in which we must consciously choose to move forward or remain stuck. In this step, we must be sure to take actions that move us forward. And if we have truly moved through the first two steps in this process, no matter how positive or negative it may seem, we can always take a positive action if we have created a positive meaning.

These first three steps of the BINK process are happening all the time and are largely unconscious, habitual reactions to the world around us. This powerful statement was actually a BINK for me as I took myself through this process! The first three steps of the BINK process are already happening in our lives; they are a habitual reaction to the world around us. So, if you consistently have a feeling of being stuck in some area of your life, it's possible to identify the disconnect and create a breakthrough. You can create a new way of looking at the information so that you can move forward.

The first and most difficult step is to make a commitment to yourself to own all of your life, choosing to be fully responsible for yourself and the results you get. Only then can you reclaim your personal life and enrich your professional one.

To quote Stephen Covey's famous suggestion, "Begin with the end in mind."

The Need for Action

As we've discussed, there is a time for dreaming, planning, and thinking; there is also a time for action. This is now. Many people who are seeking or rethinking their life purpose stay stuck in the introspection phases—or Steps 1 and 2 of the BINK process. Maybe they do this to avoid taking risks, for fear of leaving their comfort zones, to avoid disapproval, or because of any other fear, but the good thing is that you don't have to. You are here, and a richer life is soon to be had. To stop or to go in reverse is akin to staying stuck in life's rut.

I firmly believe and have found that, sometimes, the best way to find a purpose in life is to go out there and **take action**—massive action—even if we don't know what we are doing! Simply put, the best way to start is to just start.

My favorite exercise at this stage is the 5% statement, created by Nathaniel Branden, who was a pioneering figure in the self-esteem movement. It works by allowing you to start taking action in small steps. If unfolding your BINKS is akin to eating an elephant, then this exercise is simply the first bite. Trying to change completely overnight or to tackle such a potentially massive undertaking all at once, as some might suggest doing, often creates fear, uncertainty, and resistance, ultimately leading back to the "same ole, same ole."

The 5% exercise involves answering two simple questions each and every morning. Examples would be the following:

If I were to be 5% more purposeful today, I would _____.

If I were to be 5% less indecisive today, I would _____.

Then you fill in the blanks. Small steps. One bite. Just do something that is slightly challenging for yourself every day.

Another set of 5% questions could be the following:

If I were to be 5% more responsible today, I would _____.

If I were to be 5% less lazy today, I would _____.

Over time, that 5% becomes a lot more than 5%. Think of it as compounding interest; only what you're banking on is you. It builds into habits and soon will be automatic and a daily part of your routine.

The first question of the two doesn't have to change. But every morning when you wake up, you think of something different that fills in a blank and then do it! As you can see, 5% is small and harmless enough to let us overcome our fears, hurdles, and procrastination. Being flexible enough to do different things every day in pursuit of the same goal also keeps us from boredom and routine and adds an element of freshness to each and every day. Even better, it encourages us to think of new ideas to try (although we can simply do the same activity 5% more each time).

You can use this for anything you plan to do or whatever your BINKS are guiding you into: Maybe it's to start a new exercise routine, start a new business, improve your productivity at your current gig, or even improve your love life. And if 5% seems too little, don't worry: It builds up rather awesomely.

Once momentum begins, sometimes the difficulty comes in stopping!

Feed Your Body

There's so much out there these days about diet and nutrition that it's fifty shades of nutty for me to even step into this; and, yet, it's so important that it would be a shame if I didn't mention it. The truth is that you are the main source of your creativity, which means you need to feed yourself with things that are good for you.

Simply start by looking at your food—the things you are putting into your body. Are you eating a balanced diet, or are you eating junk all the time? The brutal truth is a requirement here. It's not enough to say that you ate a "healthy" dinner today if you had a candy bar and soda as a snack at 2:00 p.m.

What you eat undoubtedly determines how you're going to feel every day—tired, run-down, and lethargic, or energized, crystal clear, and focused. The choice is yours and nobody else's.

When you're fueling your body with the right foods, you'll feel awesome, and you'll have what you need to put your plan into action—the energy to create and to attack the day with vim and vigor.

My choice? My preference?

This single sentence is, for the most part, my eating mantra: *I eat fresh meats, veggies, some fruit, a little starch, and no sugar.*

That's it. No refined products and no heavy starches or breads. It works for me and keeps me on my game. The simple message is that taking action requires energy and focus, and it starts with food.

Feed Your Mind

It used to be that people thought that we needed to get into a zone or that creativity happened all on its own. I think otherwise. I think that we have the ability to spark our creative mind as we need to. In addition to feeding the body, we must learn to feed the mind, because having the ability to access that creative energy when we need it is powerful.

So how can it be done? By building creative habits into your daily life, much like a ritual. By doing so, we can schedule and thus trigger our creativity.

There's really only a single difference between those who are super creative and those who aren't: It's simply that the creative have made it part of their routine. Even if you don't think you have a creative bone in your body, simply by making it a habit, then you, too, can trigger the same things.

When you're in the habit of creativity, it will come as naturally to you as taking a breath. And then when you have a problem to solve, need an idea, or are looking for inspiration, it will be right at your fingertips—right at your beck and call. Remember, when we talk of creativity as it relates to your BINK moments, we are simply referring to the life you desire.

Here are some things you can do to feed your mind and spark your creativity:

When you combine feeding the body with feeding the mind, you'll unlock the door to creating the life you deserve, and you'll be physically and mentally ready for action.

Still with me? Great!

Let's summarize the BINK process so far. Our BINK happens, we get present and focus our attention on the moment, we get curious about what we can learn from our BINK, we get empowered and give it meaning, and then we take positive actions. We learn. We create new distinctions. We grow wise. Then lastly...

CHAPTER 15

SHARE

*There is no greater agony than bearing
an untold story inside you.*

— MAYA ANGELOU

BINK PROCESS STEP 4

In Step 4, we share the wisdom.

Think about this: If you learned some new information that
could change the world, if you had just had a huge win in your
job or your business, if you discovered something or achieved
something great, what is the first thing you would do? For
most of us, we would call someone we care about. We would
want to share the experience!

Having someone to share your wins in life with can be just as enjoyable as the wins themselves. Remember: Progress equals happiness. And, furthermore, sharing our progress increases our happiness. So, the ultimate path to fulfillment is to experience a life that allows us to progress and share that knowledge with others. When we take action, or when we figure something out, we feel great! We are programmed for growth. And sharing that experience increases our happiness. What a great system!

We are all evolutionarily programmed for growth and the desire to share that growth with others so that they may grow as well. Hoarding the wealth of knowledge within us only leads to loneliness and is just plain selfish.

When we share the wisdom, we are doing what Joseph Campbell called, in his work *The Hero's Journey*, "returning with the elixir." It's as if *you*, right now, are the hero on a journey. Now that you have slayed the dragon, overcome the battle and the challenge, and gained insight, you return home with your insight and wisdom. And, by sharing, you get to experience the joy all over again.

Purpose, as we said in the beginning, is the very reason for which something exists. Sharing your experiences, adding to the lives of others, and contributing—these not only give us a reason to exist but also the sense that our lives matter. This is where pride comes from—that sense that our pain and our struggles were for a purpose.

The vision, the contribution, and the opportunity to share

are what often pull us through. We see that heart attack victims have a higher chance of pulling through when they are married or close with their families. Successful businessmen sometimes die after retiring, but others go back to "work" because they love being a part of something. It's that sense that we matter and have something to contribute—those daily BINKS—that allow us to grow and give us something to live for!

With this sense of wisdom, as you come full circle with your experiences, you become more evolved, not through adhering to some made-up mission statement but through living and giving. And with this higher sense of awareness and purpose in life, you *open the door to what's next...*

So how exactly does one share the wisdom? I've outlined some easy ways (but not necessarily all the ways) for you to share what you've learned and make a greater impact.

Be the Model. Otherwise stated as being the person you choose to be, this is likely one of the most important things you can do to help, guide, and/or to just show others that this is all possible. Strive to be a role model, and teach by example. It's an important action and one that you can do immediately. Walk the walk, and do it visibly, so that others can see what you're doing. This goes for your spouse or loved one(s), for your kids, for family and friends, and for the folks you work with. Just showing how to do it by *being it* can be a powerful method of sharing indeed. Only you will know what this means in accordance with your BINK moment and your own sense of fulfillment and happiness. This could mean practical things, such as attending church more, uncluttering your life, or devoting time to things that matter.

Educate. Educating others is another fantastic way to share the wisdom and is actually a strong partner to "Be the Model," because by living it, you become a walking example. Think about the people you modeled yourself after—their actions, words, and legacies—and now ponder how, just by being *you*, you will indeed inadvertently educate others. Beyond that, I recommend sharing books, websites, and blogs you're reading—not in a way that states your way is the best way but, rather, just to show what you are diving into and how they might learn more and be more if they choose to (especially if they choose to follow the BINK process). Another way to educate others and thereby share your wisdom is simply to talk! Talk with them about it—again, not in a pushy way but in a way that shows how stoked you are about this life's journey and how you'd like to share what you're learning. Connection through conversation is huge.

Be patient. Patience is an essential part of sharing your wisdom. If you are in this stage, then it's because you have fully processed a BINK moment and are beginning to fully understand the deeper meaning behind it. It took time. In many instances, it took *a lot* of time. So, the message here is: As you begin to share what you've learned, be patient with others. Don't expect others to change or even to grasp the importance of this overnight just because you now do. Some folks won't learn like you did. They may have resistance to the idea or may move at a slower pace. Perhaps they understand and begin to process a BINK but stop halfway through.

In some instances, they might not want to change or support your change at all in the beginning, but later they might come around. Be patient. Being gently persistent and abundantly patient is a great way to share your newfound wisdom.

Here are some other quick and simple ways to share your wisdom and fully round out the BINK process:

- Help an entrepreneur in need, perhaps through mentoring
- Create a step-by-step instruction manual for doing something you know how to do that others would find value in
- Perform a random act of kindness; this is simple and highly impactful in some instances
- If someone asks to pay you for the random act, ask them to instead pay it forward
- Start a blog and write about your experiences
- Go to www.projectBINK.com and upload a short video of your moment
- Smile genuinely and be compassionate in all your human interactions

The last one is one of my favorites because even if one cannot think of a single way to share the wisdom of who and what they have learned and are becoming, well, we can *all* smile and treat others with compassion, and oftentimes, that is all we need to do to change somebody's life.

CHAPTER 16

ENERGY

*We keep moving forward, opening new
doors, and doing new things, because
we're curious and curiosity keeps
leading us down new paths.*

— WALT DISNEY

I do not mean to say that you won't face challenges in life, but you *will* have more clarity knowing that they are for a purpose. The promise of purpose becomes the light at the end of the tunnel.

This is what's called "the pain and the promise." We'll go through the pain of the workout if it grants us the promise of a longer, healthier life. A student will go through the pain of working on a term paper if it means getting a better job after graduation. We can endure almost any pain in life if we are clear about the promise. BINK moments happen, and we might see the pain of the moment (or the joy of it!) as a means to reach the promise of a fulfilled and purposeful life.

Can you begin to see yourself in this process? Can you begin to see how, at the very least, when the next BINK occurs—because they always do—this process is a way to decipher the "what" behind the moment?

After I figured this out, I began looking back over my life. I could then see clearly where I was stuck or the places in my life where I still needed to go through this process.

I became aware of things I wasn't fully present to.

I became aware of some disempowering meanings.

I became aware of places in my life where I had not taken action on what I knew.

I became aware of places in my life where I hadn't shared my insights.

Maybe some of you can relate to this now...

As you ponder this and begin to recall past BINK moments, remember this: We are not defined by our past but are rather being *prepared* by our past. So while they are a part of us, our past BINKS don't define who we are or what we can become.

And this applies to not only the good BINKS but to the ones that terrify us as well.

I developed Project BINK to allow myself to share what I have learned, just like Step 4 of the process mandates. And I tell you, it has led to more growth and evolution for me than anything I have ever done. Project BINK is a platform that allows you to contribute and share your stories about how BINK infused your job, your business, your home, your life, or all four, with more meaning, creating a culture and a connectedness that lead to evolution.

Today, BINK has touched over half a million lives since our 2013 launch. We have grown a community of people online who are dedicated to sharing their BINK moments, who understand just how valuable the process can be, and who are all truly inspiring individuals.

Understanding the power of our BINK moments can lead us to personally more fulfilling and joyful lives. Deploying the process in the context of your very own BINKS unfolds a deeper meaning and gives us the "what." And, on a bigger scale, processing your BINKS allows the core story of your company or organization to pull together and families to become closer all by following this process and ultimately sharing experiences that lead to growth. It isn't the purpose of life we are looking for as much as a purposeful existence. This is gained only through the experience of being alive and sharing those experiences.

CHAPTER 17

PATH

*Faith is taking the first step even when
you don't see the whole staircase.*

— MARTIN LUTHER KING, JR.

At *any point* in this process, if someone feels lost, we can see where they are on the map and where they have gotten off track, and we can create a plan to get them back on. But first please understand that some take just moments to process their BINKS, some take days, some a decade, and some an entire lifetime. If we do not fully process the BINK, instead of becoming more evolved, life seems to go round and round in a circle, much like that proverbial hamster wheel, where we are no doubt running very fast yet getting nowhere.

Perhaps we relive the same experiences in our minds over and over again, or we have the same experiences with the same types of people. We marry the same type of person, crash the same business, have the same arguments with our kids or spouses, or continue to have the same health problems—the same challenges in life. When we don't fully evolve, we don't get the lessons we are here to learn through our BINKS. We don't fully feel that sense of purpose. We feel lost. Yes, more and more of the same BINKS tend to show up if we don't learn the lesson. Then we don't progress in life, which leads to less happiness. Well, not *true* happiness, anyway.

So again, in simple terms, here is how we get off course as it relates to each step in the BINK process. Here is how we prevent ourselves from processing and honoring the BINK:

1. We distract ourselves.
2. We create a disempowering meaning—a meaning that works against us instead of for us.
3. We take no new action or a new action that is destructive to others or ourselves.
4. We don't share the wisdom. We think that the moment was meant only for us, and/or we feel alone and that life has less meaning, less purpose, and less happiness.

Getting off course, failing to process the BINK moments fully, does not allow you to open the door to what's next. You will open the door to more of the same or just keep trudging down that monotonous hallway of mediocrity or unhappiness. Your next BINK moment will be much like the last. But now that you know where you can get off course, you can use the road map to get back on track.

The BINK Road Map

Here we go, in a nutshell:

STEP 1: BE PRESENT
Ignoring the situation will not make it go away. What is something in your life—an experience in your business, relationships, or health—that you have not fully been present to?

STEP 2: REALIZE IT MEANS SOMETHING
Remember, nothing has any meaning except the meaning we give it. We can always find an empowering meaning in a situation. What did you make it mean?

STEP 3: TAKE NEW ACTION
Your actions will either move you, your job, your family, your health, and the world forward—or backward. Choose to move forward. What new action could you take today to move your life forward? And remember, no action is still action.

STEP 4: SHARE YOUR KNOWLEDGE
Share the wisdom gained though experience. A sense of contribution, along with growth, leads to a higher sense of purpose. What is your story? What is an experience in your life or a lesson learned through trial and error that could help others? Go ahead and share it!

When you do this, you open the door to what's next and move toward living your purpose. Our lives are built through experiences, triumphs, and lessons learned. When shared, this leads us to growth and propels our own personal evolution. It leads us to be more effective, happy, fulfilled, and successful, all based on our experiences—our BINKS! And the purpose you discover is yours because the experiences are yours. This is *your* life, *your* purpose, and no one else's. Now when you seek out new experiences, you realize BINKS are happening all around you. And you don't have to go to the moon to find them. They are happening right here in your home and in your business.

There is a VITALITY, a life FORCE, an ENERGY, a QUICKENING that is translated through YOU into ACTION, and because there is only one of you in all time, this expression is UNIQUE. And if you block it, it will never exist through any other medium and will be lost.

— MARTHA GRAHAM

CHAPTER 18

CHOICE

*The brain is a wonderful organ; it
starts working the moment you
get up in the morning and does not
stop until you get into the office.*

— ROBERT FROST

BINKS aren't always these huge, obvious, life-altering moments like some of the ones we've touched on so far. They can also be the little things.

Let's talk about a real-life BINK and how it can apply to you whether you own a business, work at a business, or have had an experience with a business. That's pretty much everyone, no? Let's explore a BINK that is likely happening in any company at any given time on any given day, and you will see how the BINK process relates. We'll discover how something as simple as a customer service call can change a company culture, a bottom line, management, customers, and the success of any organization from top to bottom.

Imagine that a customer service rep is on the phone with a customer and the call ends in an unresolved disagreement. It happens...or should we say, BINK happens!

This phone call is a BINK moment.

Here is what we often see and a great example of how *not* to process a BINK.

STEP 1: GET PRESENT: Often, the stressful interaction leads the rep to go take a break, maybe smoke a cigarette, have something to eat, or search the Internet. In other words, they dissociate, tune out, and distract themselves. To them, it's almost like it never happened.

Or perhaps they *do* get present to the call, but as they move immediately into **STEP 2: EMOTION AND MEANING**, they make the call mean something negative. Remember, we get to choose what things mean, and nothing has any meaning except the meaning we give it. They could make their BINK mean, "I shouldn't be working here. Nobody appreciates me. All customers are jerks. Something is wrong with me, wrong with the job, and wrong with the customer." They simply have a negative mental/emotional response—a negative meaning. But it's impossible to create positive results while filled with negative emotions.

Then, with this negative meaning, they move to **STEP 3: ACTION**. Here we notice the *negative* actions.

Maybe the rep quits, is short with the next customer, doesn't hit their quota, gives up, and becomes jealous of others in the workplace, or their attitude suffers and morale worsens.

In this case, **STEP 4** is the worst. Usually, it doesn't get to this point, but it does happen. **STEP 4** is where we share the wisdom, remember? But for *this* individual, sharing the experience is not a good thing. They turn into a bad apple, sharing negative talk around the watercooler. They gossip, complain, share what they learned in a negative way, and project blame. This kills company culture.

Instead of opening the door to what's next, these actions only open the door to more of the same. The person doesn't get the lesson. They don't hear the call. They don't evolve in their career or in their lives. If there are enough of these folks in an organization, it will not evolve either.

No evolution and no growth. And that which isn't growing is _____. That's right, it's dying.

Can you now imagine for a second how the *customer* on the other end of the phone is processing this? Think about it: The BINK goes two ways, and if you are the customer, then it's *you* who also gets to choose the meaning and the action and to share some wisdom. What an interesting thing this is, right? Think about these types of interactions in your personal life now. The phone calls or conversations with friends, family, or others where we've felt it could have, or should have, gone differently.

So now let's talk about the BINK shift.

CHAPTER 19

REDEEMED

*Far and away the best prize that life
has to offer is the chance to work
hard at work worth doing.*

— THEODORE ROOSEVELT

Let's look at the same exact call, but this time, the customer service rep understands the BINK process. We will notice a very different outcome—a very different result.

In **STEP 1: GET PRESENT,** the rep simply gets present, recognizing that they just had a BINK moment. They don't ignore the situation; they indeed see things as they truly are (not worse than they are) and just take a moment to actually be present in the moment.

In **STEP 2: EMOTION AND MEANING.** They make the moment mean something empowering, perhaps learning what not to say. They think of how they could have handled it differently, setting up a time to listen to the call again or talk to a supervisor about it. They look to find a way they could have created a different result, *or* they realize that the customer was simply in a bad mood, and they commit to do better on the next call. They actually take a moment to think about how the call could have gone better, envision this, and then seek to make that positive vision a reality.

Then, in **STEP 3: ACTION,** the rep takes the new insight and applies it. They learn a new strategy and utilize the distinction learned on the last call for the next one. They have now learned a better way to handle similar customer situations and apply this knowledge to future calls, *or* they actually call the customer back and make a second attempt to create a positive experience.

In **STEP 4,** this is where the rep shares the wisdom. Perhaps they speak up on a team conference call to talk about how they turned around a difficult client and went the extra mile, or they have a new distinction that they may want to take home and share with their kids. Once experience is gained and action applied, there will be successes along the way. Sharing these wins so that others can benefit creates team players and a winning environment.

This is opening the door to what's next. These distinctions create the kind of culture that allows companies, relationships, teams, and individuals to evolve and grow.

The customer service rep we just discussed successfully opened the door to what's next. And for that person, it could be a raise, a promotion, or opening his or her own consulting firm or partnership. The sky's the limit!

In the first example, the person we spoke about received more of the same. Job after job, with no evolution or growth, that feeling of being stuck persisted.

Although these are the extremes, people get stuck at every level. Contribution and wisdom sharing creates a team environment, a sense of belonging, and a sense of purpose.

BINKS are happening in our companies, in our friendships, in our homes, and in our health.

BINKS can be small, seemingly insignificant experiences such as these, or they can be tremendous losses: an argument with your spouse, a negative change in the economy or industry, or a miscommunication with your child.

BINKS give us the signs on life's road map to navigate life's experiences big and small. They allow us a process to move forward in life, to grow, and to live lives of purpose.

BINKS are life-changing moments that open the door to what's next.

Now, I invite you to think about a BINK in your life: a moment in which you got present, clear, and empowered; a moment in which you took positive action and shared the wisdom; a moment that led you to this place in your life today...right here, right now, with this book open in front of you.

Perhaps it's an experience where you have come full circle or perhaps one where you can now see where you may be stuck. And this isn't just in your personal life or in business; it could be at home or in your health.

So, what have been your BINKS?

Write down one or two BINKS—positive or negative—that have impacted you personally or professionally.

CHAPTER 20

MELT

*I learned that courage was not the absence
of fear, but the triumph over it. The
brave man is not he who does not feel
afraid, but he who conquers that fear.*

— NELSON MANDELA

My family and some close friends were all on vacation in Mexico. It was a pretty warm and humid day, and we were all in our bathing suits, psyching ourselves up for the zip line excursion we had just signed up for.

The line to get on the ride was a long one, but through conversation, telling jokes, and talking about our plans to head to Señor Frogs for a margarita later that evening, the time flew by. Before we knew it, it was our turn to strap into the harnesses.

My husband snapped in, and my best friend's daughters were snapped in too. Then it was my turn, and the zip line guy hesitated and pointed to the other line. The other line was the harness for "big" people, and he said in broken English that I was "too much"—that I was "mucho" for the line.

Mortified? Embarrassed? Hurt? Sad? You might ask if I felt these things, and I would reply, "It was all these things and more, wrapped up like a roll of nickels in a sock and swung into my gut. My heart. Shit, it hit me in my freakin' soul!"

But I smiled because I didn't want my husband, my son, or my best friends in the whole wide world to know what just hit me. I took a deep breath, smiled, and said, "See you guys at the end!" I sounded as cheerful as possible to hide the truth of what I was feeling.

At the time, it hurt...really badly. And, later, I realized I had experienced a BINK to the 10th level, if that even exists. I think it does. The zip line ride started, and I was floating down, thinking,

Hell, I have done my New Year's resolutions...nine years in a row now...

I have hired a personal trainer. I just haven't shown up.

I have bought "healthy" foods and watched them get moldy.

I reached the bottom without even realizing the ride was over.

I had become so wrapped up in my own head that I missed the ride.

But by the time I reached the bottom, I felt different.

I zip-lined the afternoon away.

I went to Señor Frogs and had margaritas.

I fell asleep that night with my husband, who always loved me and loves me for who I am.

And then I got home.

And made a massive change.

I share this story today because I wish that I had decided long ago to just commit and make the right choices. I share this story today because I can now see how that BINK helped me to grow, evolve, and to find *my purpose*. I see how I must now shed my fears, destroy my vulnerabilities, crush my beliefs that I was alone in this, and tell you that I am new.

From 247 to 175. And counting. Fuck that weight.

I refuse to let life happen to me. I now *choose* to make *me* happen to life. And it's powerful. Liberating. Sexy. Invigorating.

My husband always told me I was beautiful, and I believed

him. Now he says I'm beautiful, and not only do I believe him, I believe *me*.

Did my BINK change me? Well, that's debatable.

I like to think that my BINK happened. And I finally listened after getting really present to the whole moment. I gave it a new meaning. I acted. As far as sharing the knowledge, well, that's where I had the most difficulty. Truth be told, I really felt that my BINK was a private matter. Sure, I'd seen the Weight Watchers commercials with the big-name stars and then the average moms who spritely show off the before and after pictures. But that's not me. As I considered the BINK process, I realized that my chokepoint was Step 4. It's where my fear really reared its ugly head. But I finally decided that if I was going to grow and truly evolve, then I must share. And share I did. On social media, with my friends, and with friends of friends of friends, I shared my journey, my struggles, and yes, I shared my wins, and I should say I am better for it.

CHAPTER 21

YOU

*Life isn't about finding yourself. Life
is about creating yourself.*

— GEORGE BERNARD SHAW

The purpose of life is evolution, and BINKS are your guide. A
life of purpose is a life filled with experiences.

All BINKS fall into one of two broad categories—obvious or
subtle—and, from there, they cascade into a variety of areas.
As we said earlier, it could have been a big BINK or a little BINK,
a health BINK or an emotional BINK, a relationship BINK or
a business BINK.

No matter where you are in your life, you can now see that
there *is a process*. Awareness is the first step to improving or

changing anything and knowing the road ahead. And having the ability to anticipate keeps us from getting stuck. Again, it can take a moment, a year, or twenty years to process your BINKS and come full circle, evolved, and ready for what is coming your way in your next cycle of growth. But it will come. It is through our experiences, through our actions, that we find it. Yes, it's as if the universe is speaking to us *right now*. All we have to do is listen.

If you want to have a full and rewarding life, you must increase your references. It is only by pursuing ideas, fully engaging in the experience of life, and creating distinctions from those moments that we grow and evolve.

Your life's purpose isn't going to just sneak up and grab you. You have to seek it out.

And realize your purpose is always growing and evolving. The person that doesn't embrace this concept will one day ask what it all meant and ask why they didn't do something sooner. The great relationships that don't grow together will eventually grow apart. The successful companies of today that do not evolve will not be in business ten years from now.

Seek not just to find your purpose but also to live more purposefully. See every day as an opportunity to grow. And now that you have a map, you don't have to get lost along the way. If you, your company, or your relationship is stuck—if you feel stuck in *any* area—I invite you to listen, to get present, to develop more empowering meanings, to take more action, and to give back by sharing what you learn along the way. This will open the door to what's next. This will open the door to a life of growth, evolution, progress, purpose, and happiness.

CHAPTER 22

TODAY

You have brains in your head. You have
feet in your shoes. You can steer yourself in
any direction you choose. You're on your
own, and you know what you know. And
you are the guy who'll decide where to go.

— DR. SEUSS

As a final note, I want to say that BINKS rarely appear in our lives as one-offs. Instead, they are often a series—a wave, if you will—of events, moments, and choices that each has the power to impact or direct our lives in a different way. Every BINK in the series is as important as the next, and every one is meaningful, even if it might not feel that way at the time.

It was the fallout from my accident that taught me this inescapable truth. I was lying on the ground, feeling fully present to the moment as the pain washed through my body, my leg crushed under 225lbs of weight. As a trained ER nurse, I thought my femur had been broken, if only because of the loud snapping sound—like a tree branch breaking—that had rung out on impact. Thankfully, I had not broken a bone but, rather, had sheared the tendon and entire quad muscle right off my knee. The bar had rather violently "removed" the muscle cleanly away. The now "freed" muscle had essentially rolled up, like an old school rolling window blind, into my upper right thigh.

My injury required reconstructive surgery and months of physical therapy for me to essentially learn how to walk again. Was I in pain? Yep. Did I want to quit? No question. Was I asking "Why me?" more than once a day? Absolutely. In short, the healing process was one gigantic and never-ending BINK moment.

I had to relearn even the most basic skills: putting my pants on in reverse order, using the potty, and dealing with numerous doctors' appointments and a radical change to my life. Each day was a new day full of challenges, and it was because of the BINK process that I was able to approach each day fresh, alive, and knowing that, in the end, I would persevere. The entirety of the healing took easily one year before I was able to truly put on my running shoes and go for a run without aid, pain, or assistance.

One year. But that run was easily one of the most incredible experiences of my life. Instead of the arrogance with which

I had stepped up to my weight rack a year earlier, this time, I was bursting with gratitude. I was joyfully aware of the sun on my face and the wind at my back. I felt thankful for what my body was able to do, supporting my weight and pushing me forward, as every piece worked as a whole. I felt present and connected to the moment. Wiping the big smile off my face would have been impossible.

And to celebrate? Well, I decided to enter an Ironman triathlon and promptly began the next phase of my life. I completed Ironman Arizona in November 2014.

Becoming present, finding an empowering meaning, taking new and massive action, and then sharing what I learned transformed me. This mantra—this process—has allowed me, and will allow you, to overcome and to create a life of deeper meaning and true purpose...the life you deserve.

CHAPTER 23

TOMORROW

Accept what is, let go of what was,
and have faith in what will be.

— SONIA RICOTTI

Final note.

I truly believe you're at the start of an incredible journey. It's truly up to you to now decide:

Will you set this on the bookshelf, say "interesting read," and then breeze into tomorrow hoping to find fulfillment?

Or will you set this book down and make a commitment to yourself to think about BINKS in a whole new way and see just how they can fully impact your life?

Based on my experience, if you fully embrace the process and the idea that it truly is about the BINK moments that give us purpose and direction, then you will indeed be more fulfilled, find real happiness, and lead a life of deep purpose.

(But that's just me.)

I sincerely hope that this book has been a BINK for you and that you now feel you have an important tool to move you forward toward your purpose in life—a life of new and exciting adventures. I would also like to thank you personally for picking this up and reading it today, as each time you feel inspired, each time you share your BINK story or purpose with me and with the world, you help me fulfill my own purpose and mission in life. So, in a way, you have already shared your wisdom.

I invite you to join the BINK Community at www.projectBINK.com and easily connect with us through social media, as well as on the site. Also, for some quick daily wisdom in your inbox, sign up for our daily BINK Boost.

Now, think BINK, and go open the door to what's next!

Cheers to a beautiful life.

— RICK

CHAPTER 24

MINDSHARE

*It is in your moments of decision
that your destiny is shaped.*

— TONY ROBBINS

Feedback and Food for Thought

*Consider the following questions and thought provokers below. Have
they applied to you? Could they? I'd love to get a dialogue going, and
if you are so inclined, I'd also love to hear back from you. Pick your
top three provokers below and write me back. Share your answers
and your thoughts. Email them to mindshare@projectbink.com.*

1. What does a BINK mean to you?
   - Finding what's next
   - A life-changing experience that sets a new path
   - An event that has stopped you in your tracks and caused you to reevaluate what's important

2. When have you had a BINK that got your attention and impacted you?

3. Did you act on the BINK? Did you do something different as a result?
   - If no, why not?
   - If yes, what happened?

4. Why do you think we get BINKS? Where are they coming from? Why do they happen?
   - ReDirect...ReGround...ReFresh...ReGret...ReMind... ReNotice...ReSet

5. Did you ever ignore a BINK? Why?
   - Give examples: Perhaps you had a great business idea, got feedback from someone, and didn't start.

6. Who is someone who delivered a BINK? Who opened your eyes to something?

7. Who is this person and what was the situation?

8. When have *you* delivered a BINK?

9. Were you reluctant?

10. Did you wonder if it was your right?

11. How was it delivered, and were they receptive?

12. Do you have a favorite resource? A favorite quote? Something that keeps your BINK at the forefront?

13. Do you have any BINK recommendations?

14. What could I include on the blog, website, or book that you would find interesting?

How did you put your BINK into action?

AUTHOR

It's not really about me. It's about us.

I'd love to stay connected:

twitter.com/planetboyrn

facebook.com/ProjectBINK

Me: **www.itsrickmartinez.com**

Us: **www.FightTheManana.com**

BINK: **www.projectbink.com**

www.ingramcontent.com/pod-product-compliance
Lightning Source LLC
LaVergne TN
LVHW051601080426
835510LV00020B/3083